PHARAOH PUZZLED.

The story about Pharaoh and Joseph is taken from Genesis, chapter 41.

So Pharaoh sent for Joseph, and he was quickly brought from the dungeon. When he had shaved and changed his clothes, he came before Pharaoh.

Pharaoh said to Joseph, "I had a dream, and no-one can interpret it. But I have heard it said of you that when you hear a dream you can interpret it."

"I cannot do it," Joseph replied to Pharaoh, "but God will give Pharaoh the answer he desires."

"It is just as I said to Pharaoh: God has shown Pharaoh what he is about to do. Seven years of great abundance are coming throughout the land of Egypt, but seven years of famine will follow them. Then all the abundance in Egypt will be forgotten, and the famine will ravage the land. The abundance in the land will not be remembered, because the famine that follows it will be so severe. The reason the dream was given to Pharaoh in two forms is that the matter has been firmly decided by God, and God will do it soon."

The plan seemed good to Pharaoh and to all his officials. So Pharaoh asked them, "Can we find anyone like this man, one in whom is the spirit of God?"

Then Pharaoh said to Joseph, "Since God has made all this known to you, there is no-one so discerning and wise as you. You shall be in charge of my palace, and all my people are to submit to your orders. Only with respect to the throne will I be greater than you."

Genesis 41:14-16; 28-32; 37-40, NIV

Why Was Pharaoh Puzzled?

Published by Scandinavia Publishing House
Nørregade 32, DK-1165 Copenhagen K.
Tel.: (45) 33140091 Fax: (45) 33320091
E-Mail: scanpub1@post4.tele.dk

Copyright © 1996, Pauline Youd
Copyright © on artwork 1996, Daughters of St. Paul
Original English edition published by Pauline Books & Media,
50 Saint Paul's Avenue, Boston, USA
Scripture quotations are from the Holy Bible, New International Version,
Copyright © 1973, 1978, International Bible Society
Design by Ben Alex
Produced by Scandinavia Publishing House
Printed in Singapore.
ISBN 87 7247 041 0

All rights reserved. No part of this book may be reproduced or utilized
in any form or by any means, electronic or mechanical, including
photocopying, recording, or by any information storage and retrieval
system, without permission in writing from the publisher.

WHY WAS PHARAOH PUZZLED?

By Pauline Youd
Illustrated by Elaine Garvin

SCANDINAVIA

Pharaoh had a very
strange dream.
It woke him up.
  The dream puzzled him.
What did it mean?
  Pharaoh didn't know, so he
went back to sleep.

But Pharaoh dreamed another strange dream that woke him up.

Pharaoh was very puzzled.

He called his wise men and told them his dreams.

"What do my dreams mean?" he asked.

The wise men didn't know.
"There is a man named Joseph who knows what dreams mean," one wise man said.

Pharaoh called Joseph in and told him his dreams.

"I dreamed about seven fat cows and seven skinny cows," Pharaoh said. "But the seven skinny cows ate up the seven fat cows. Then I went back to sleep and dreamed another dream.

"I dreamed about seven fat ears of corn and seven skinny ears of corn.

"But the seven skinny ears of corn ate up the seven fat ears of corn. I am puzzled. Can you tell me what my dreams mean?"

"God helps me know what dreams mean," said Joseph. "The two dreams mean the same thing. The seven fat cows and the seven fat ears of corn mean seven years with plenty of food.

"The seven skinny cows and the seven skinny ears of corn mean seven years when there will be no food. You need someone to collect food during the seven good years. Then you will have food to give the people during the seven bad years."

"I will do what you say," said Pharaoh. "Your God has made you very wise."

Now Pharaoh could sleep well. He wasn't puzzled any more.

11

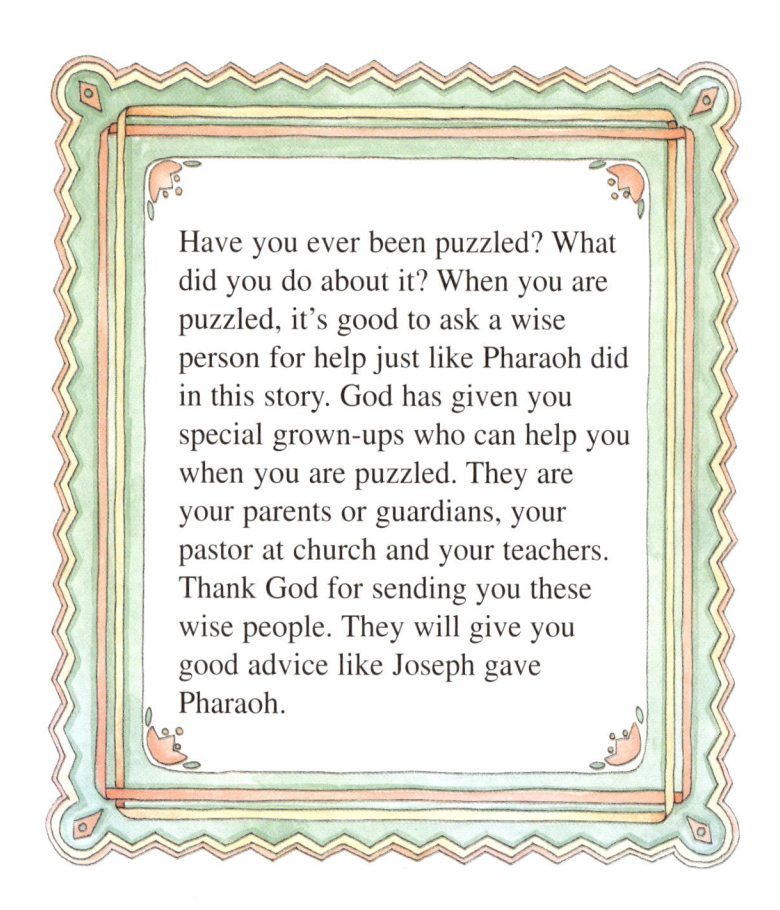

Have you ever been puzzled? What did you do about it? When you are puzzled, it's good to ask a wise person for help just like Pharaoh did in this story. God has given you special grown-ups who can help you when you are puzzled. They are your parents or guardians, your pastor at church and your teachers. Thank God for sending you these wise people. They will give you good advice like Joseph gave Pharaoh.

13

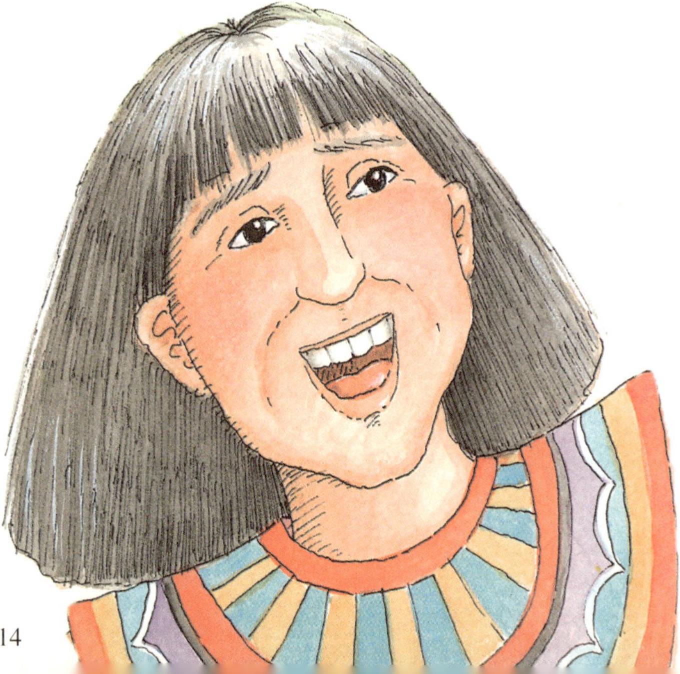

"Since God has made all this known to you, there is no-one so discerning and wise as you. You shall be in charge of my palace, and all my people are to submit to your orders. Only with respect to the throne will I be greater than you."

Genesis 41:39

WONDER BOOKS
Lessons to learn from 12 Bible characters

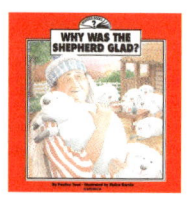

WHY WAS THE SHEPHERD GLAD?	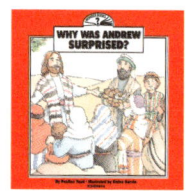 **WHY WAS ANDREW SURPRISED?**	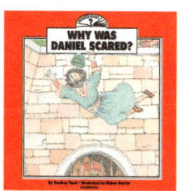 **WHY WAS DANIEL SCARED?**	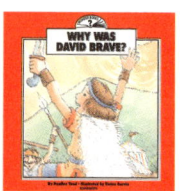 **WHY WAS DAVID BRAVE?**
God's Love	Self-giving	Prayer Overcomes Fear	Praising God
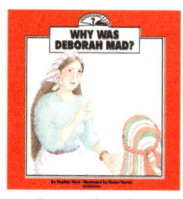 **WHY WAS DEBORAH MAD?**	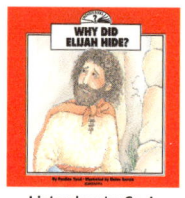 **WHY DID ELIJAH HIDE?**	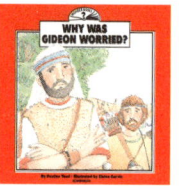 **WHY WAS GIDEON WORRIED?**	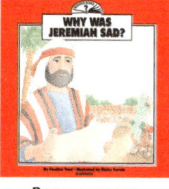 **WHY WAS JEREMIAH SAD?**
Prayer Obtains Wisdom	Listening to God	Trust	Perseverance
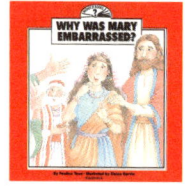 **WHY WAS MARY EMBARRASSED?**	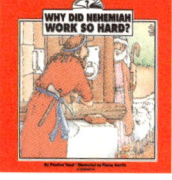 **WHY DID NEHEMIAH WORK SO HARD?**	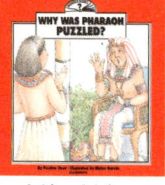 **WHY WAS PHARAOH PUZZLED?**	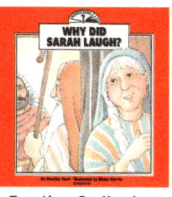 **WHY DID SARAH LAUGH?**
Loving Obedience	Persistence	Asking Advice	Trusting God's plan